AN IMAGINATION LIBRARY SERIES

Colors of the Sea

CORAL REEF HUNTERS

Eric Ethan and Marie Bearanger

Gareth Stevens Publishing
MILWAUKEE

For a free color catalog describing Gareth Stevens Publishing's list of high-quality books and multimedia programs, call 1-800-542-2595 (USA) or 1-800-461-9120 (Canada). Gareth Stevens Publishing's Fax: (414) 225-0377.
See our catalog, too, on the World Wide Web: http://gsinc.com

Library of Congress Cataloging-in-Publication Data

Ethan, Eric.
  Coral reef hunters / Eric Ethan and Marie Bearanger.
    p. cm. — (Colors of the sea)
  Includes index.
  Summary: Describes hunting techniques used by predators that live in and around coral reefs.
  ISBN 0-8368-1739-7 (lib. bdg.)
  1. Coral reef animals—Behavior—Juvenile literature. 2. Predatory marine animals—Juvenile literature. 3. Coral reef fishes—Behavior—Juvenile literature. 4. Predation (Biology)—Juvenile literature. [1. Coral reef animals. 2. Marine animals. 3. Predatory animals.] I. Bearanger, Marie. II. Title. III. Series: Ethan, Eric. Colors of the sea.
QL125.E84 1997
597.177'89—dc21
               96-37057

First published in North America in 1997 by
Gareth Stevens Publishing
1555 North RiverCenter Drive, Suite 201
Milwaukee, WI 53212 USA

This edition © 1997 by Gareth Stevens, Inc. Adapted from *Colors of the Sea* © 1992 by Elliott & Clark Publishing, Inc., Washington, D.C. Text by Owen Andrews. Photographs © 1992 by W. Gregory Brown. Additional end matter © 1997 by Gareth Stevens, Inc.

Text: Eric Ethan, Marie Bearanger
Page layout: Eric Ethan, Helene Feider
Cover design: Helene Feider
Series design: Shari Tikus

The publisher wishes to acknowledge the encouragement and support of Glen Fitzgerald.

Printed in the United States of America

1 2 3 4 5 6 7 8 9 01 00 99 98 97

TABLE OF CONTENTS

WHAT IS A PREDATOR?

In what is known as the **food chain**, each living thing survives by feeding on the next living thing in the chain. An animal that feeds on another animal in the chain is a **predator**. At the top of the ocean food chain are the large predators, such as sharks.

Many kinds of sea creatures, including fish, make their homes near coral reefs. Most fish are predators. Bigger fish eat smaller fish. The smallest sea creatures in the food chain often live on plants like **algae**.

A lizardfish, *Synodus variegatus*, preys on a smaller fish — the false cleaner blenny, *Aspidontus taeniatus*.

HOW DO FISH HUNT?

During the hunt, predator fish move quickly. Some fish can go from a standstill to full speed in 1/20 of a second. Fish do not chase their **prey** a long distance before catching it. This would use up too much energy.

Fish do not have hands to hold their food like humans do. They must swallow their prey in one or two gulps. This is why fish almost always eat fish smaller than they are.

It is rare to actually see one fish eat another because it happens so quickly.

The longnose hawkfish, *Oxycirrhites typus*, has large eyes that help it find prey.

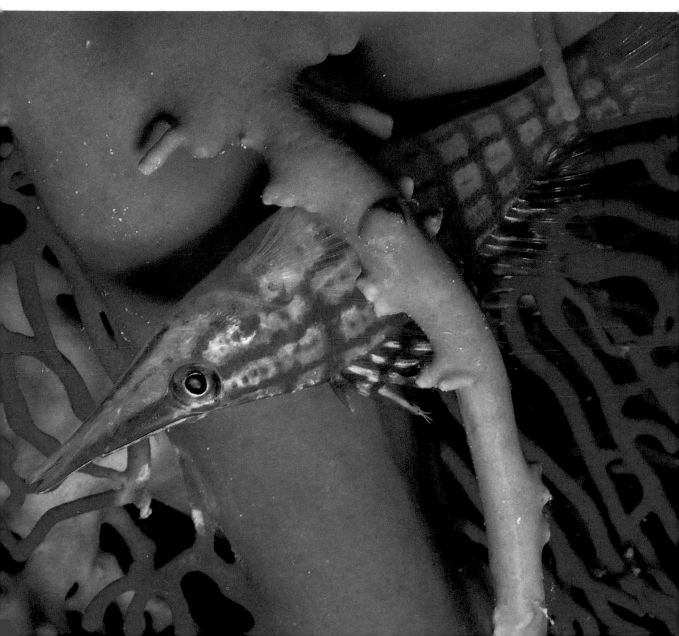

WHAT IS CAMOUFLAGE?

Some predators **ambush** their prey. They hide until the prey comes close. Then they quickly try to grab it. **Camouflage** helps fish hide by allowing them to blend into the surroundings or by disguising them as another object.

For example, stonefish and scorpionfish are covered with small patches of bright colors that look like algae. When they lie still near a reef, they look like the algae. Small fish will swim quite near and be eaten because they do not see the danger.

This spotfin lionfish, *Pterois antennata*, is well camouflaged when it floats near brightly colored coral.

Predator fish that do not have camouflage coloring are still able to hide in coral reefs. The reefs have various holes, tunnels, and crannies in which predator fish hide before ambushing prey.

Moray eels are expert at hiding in coral reefs. These long, slender sea creatures can reach 1-3 feet (30-90 centimeters) in length. They back into tunnels in the coral and hide. When prey comes near, they strike quickly.

Moray eels do not have good eyesight. They have four nostrils to find prey by scent.

The goldentail moray, *Gymnothorax miliaris*, is a fierce-looking eel.

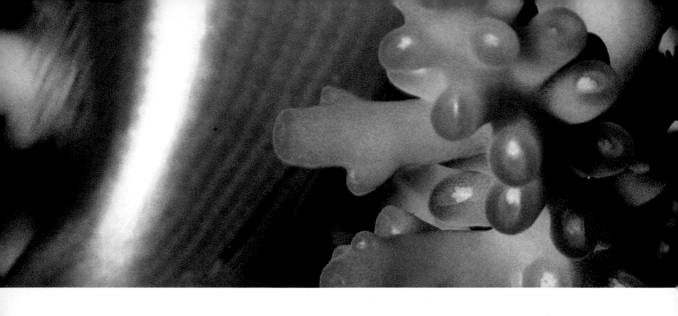

HUNTING TERRITORY

Predator fish that hide in the coral reef usually have a definite hunting **territory**. This is an area each fish defends against others.

Smaller predators like the hawkfish have territories at the top of coral growth. They swoop down on their prey like the hawks for which they are named.

The arc-eyed hawkfish, *Paracirrhites arcuatus*, remains motionless at the top of new coral growth for hours while hunting prey.

SCAVENGERS OF THE SEA

Some sea creatures are **scavengers.** They live by eating leftover bits of prey hunted by other fish. Scavengers help keep the oceans clean.

One example is the remora fish. It hitches a ride on the back of a shark, eating bits of fish the shark does not swallow. Many crabs search the seafloor for pieces of fish dropped by other predators.

The red hermit crab, *Paguristes cadenati*, is a scavenger.

DO SHARKS LIVE NEAR REEFS?

A few sharks, such as the gray reef shark, are often found near coral reefs. But most of the over three hundred species of sharks are found farther out in deeper waters.

Unlike most fish, sharks can prey on sea creatures their own size. Their strong jaws and sharp teeth make it possible to bite prey into pieces small enough to swallow.

The Caribbean reef shark, *Carcharhinus perezi*, makes its home near the coral reef.

16

The numbers of sharks around the world are decreasing. In some areas, this is due to **overfishing** by **commercial** fishermen. The fishermen believe that sharks make their catches smaller, so the fishermen kill the sharks. But the truth is sharks have little effect on the number of fish in the ocean.

Some sharks have been killed by people because of the incorrect belief that sharks prey on humans. When sharks attack people, it is usually because they have mistaken them for sea animals, such as seals. If a shark bites a human, the shark usually does not eat the human. Scientists believe sharks do not like the taste of humans.

Compared to a shark, the red-spotted hawkfish, *Amblycirrhites pinos*, is a very small hunter. It lunges at prey from the top of the coral reef.

ARMORED SEA CREATURES

Only a few **reptiles** inhabit the ocean. The most common are sea turtles. Most sea turtles do best in deep water, so they live far from shore. But in the South Pacific, the hawksbill turtle is commonly found near coral reefs.

Many turtles eat fish and other sea creatures. Near the reef, the hawksbill turtle feeds on sponges and jellyfish.

The hawksbill turtle was much more common in the past. But many have been captured because of the hawksbill's beautiful shell, and divers rarely see this turtle anymore. It is now a **threatened** species.

The hawksbill turtle, *Eretmochelys imbricata*, makes its home near coral reefs in the South Pacific.

THE MOST DANGEROUS PREDATORS

Humans are the most dangerous of the ocean predators. By the early 1900s, humans had over-fished several kinds of whales into **extinction**. Even today, the world's nations do not all agree about putting an end to whaling.

The entire fishing industry is suffering because of overfishing. Large fishing fleets and huge drift nets have resulted in a shortage of fish in areas around the world that once had an abundance. The northeast coast of North America was once a bountiful commercial fishing area. Now it has poor harvests, and fishing is limited. Humans must learn to conserve the ocean's **resources** before even more of its species become extinct.

GLOSSARY

algae (AL-jee) — Living water plants that are food for many sea creatures.

ambush (AM-bush) — To attack with surprise from a hiding place.

camouflage (KAM-oh-flazh) — Shapes or colors on an animal's body that disguise the animal and help it hide.

commercial (kah-MER-shull) — A business that is operated for profit.

extinction (ex-TINK-shun) — The process of totally destroying.

food chain (FOOD chane) — The natural process by which each plant and animal in the series feeds on another member of the series to survive.

overfishing (OH-ver-FISH-ing) — Taking fish from an area beyond its capacity.

predator (PRED-a-ter) — An animal that lives by feeding on other animals.

prey (PRAY) — An animal hunted by another animal for food.

reptile (REP-tile) — A cold-blooded animal that creeps or crawls on the ground. It is covered with scales or horned plates.

resource (REE-sorse) — A valuable or desirable object.

scavenger (SKAV-en-jer) — An animal that eats matter that is dead or discarded.

territory (TARE-ih-tor-ee) — A particular area that is occupied by an animal or group of animals and defended against intruders.

threatened (THRET-ened) — Nearing the condition of being endangered.

WEB SITES

http://www.blacktop.com/coralforest/

http://planet-hawaii.com/sos/coralreef.html

PLACES TO WRITE

The Cousteau Society, Inc.
870 Greenbrier Circle, Suite 402
Chesapeake, VA 23320

Environmental Protection Agency
Oceans and Coastal Protection Division
401 M Street SW
Washington, D.C. 20460

Greenpeace (USA)
1436 U Street NW
Washington, D.C. 20009

Greenpeace (Canada)
2623 West Fourth Avenue
Vancouver, British Columbia V6K 1P8

Greenpeace Foundation
185 Spadina Avenue, Sixth Floor
Toronto, Ontario M5T 2C6

Center for Marine Conservation
1725 DeSales Street, Suite 500
Washington, D.C. 20036

National Geographic Society
17th and M Streets NW
Washington, D.C. 20036

INDEX